PRINCE RUPERT'S DROP

Prince Rupert's Drop

Jane Draycott

Oxford*Poets*

CARCANET

First published in Great Britain in 1999 by Oxford University Press
and in the United States by Oxford University Press Inc., New York

This impression first published in 2004 by
Carcanet Press Limited
Alliance House
Cross Street
Manchester M2 7AQ

A CIP catalogue record for this book is available from
the British Library
ISBN 1 903039 75 4

The publisher acknowledges financial assistance from
Arts Council England

Typeset by George Hammond Design
Printed and bound in England by SRP Ltd, Exeter

For Norman, Holly, and Sophie,
and in memory of
Nigel and Peggy

ACKNOWLEDGEMENTS

Acknowledgements are due to the editors of the following publications in which some of these poems appeared: *British Archaeology*, *The Devil*, *Fatchance*, *The Forward Book of Poetry 1998*, *Greek Gifts* (Smith/Doorstop), *The Independent*, *Jugular Defences* (The Oscars Press), *London Magazine*, *The Long Pale Corridor* (Bloodaxe Books), *The North*, *Oxford Poetry*, *Poetry London Newsletter*, *Remembered Place* (The Housman Society), *The Rialto*, *The Silkies* (Poetry Society), *South*, *This Is*, *Virago New Poets*, *Word for Word* (Blackwells/Southern Arts), the *1997 Dulwich Festival Anthology*, and *The Bridport Prize Anthology 1998*.

Eight of these poems appeared in the pamphlet *No Theatre* (Smith/Doorstop) which was a first-stage winner in The Poetry Business Competition 1996.

'Prince Rupert's Drop' and 'Wedding Breakfast' are from *A Glass Case*, a BBC R3 commission broadcast in 1996, and 'Silence, Drift, Aeroplane' is from *Sea Green I*, joint winner of Radio 3's Poem for Radio Competition 1997, both co-written with Elizabeth James.

The St Christina poems are from a collaborative collection *Christina the Astonishing* (Two Rivers Press, 1998) co-written with Lesley Saunders, with images by Peter Hay.

CONTENTS

When I woke, the darkest dreams continued
. . . I was forced to travel

Rimbaud, 'Une saison en enfer'

There's a face I see in the wells, sits
like a crow on my shoulder. Home-sick
and sick of home, these small fires
I tread—the way these strangers
build their walls, and the unfamiliar flies.

Stopping to sleep, I dream the bare song
under my heels: of the rising before dawn,
the ashes dead in the grate, and the town
rolling away at my feet. In the morning
the black trees have vanished from the field.

I walk the dry hand of the earth and in that oven
burn away my name and the place that I was born

Silence, Drift, Aeroplane

Silence, drift, aeroplane: on the day they come
you will be mending nets along the raspberry wall.

In the small light of the kitchen rain,
the wind will sharpen his knives. Ash and apple,
full fathom five by the cathedral clock
and all souls lost across the lawns of the parish.

That night, sailing your mattress of crossed wires,
you will pass in the street other boats
you seem to know—*The Kiss of the Sun
for Pardon, The Rose Amongst the Thorns.*

Then the eye of the day will open,
you will be small again, the drowning airman
in the compost heap gone home. In the stubble
fields the waters rise, the sheep drift and bob.

Braving the Dark

*in memory of my brother Nigel
and for the staff of London Lighthouse*

1 Search

Passive, your glove allows me to enter
its five black-soft tunnels:
the tips however remained uninhabited,
your fingers having been longer than mine.

The words you typed and left, expecting to return,
file out across their electronic lawn.
I caress them with the cursor, like a medium
stroking the table at a seance.

At your pain on the answerphone tape my voice
sticks, as at the gaps in a linguaphone lesson.
In tears, I sort the wafers of your clothes for friends—
straightjacketed in card you watch, and seem unmoved.

At last day buckles and, awake in bed, I find you:
the deadweight limbs we turned two-hourly
and powdered to protect your baffled skin
become my own, crook'd flat along the sheet

and from the soft lame triangle that your mouth became
you breathe our childhood out upon my pillow.
Wearing the features of our father,
your frightened face sleeps inside mine.

3

II Dream

The Vicar arrives by rowing-boat,
vampire-stalks our wet front path
and batlike settles out his cloak
for The Consolation of the Bereaved

(flashback to our mother's funeral
when we remarked how very like a piece of theatre
funerals are, as his hand webbed out
a fraction on his Book of Common Prayer).

His head is tortoising out to kiss me.
I am trying to explain my disinclination
to dance, when you appear suddenly from the lounge,
perfectly whole, to save me.

Outside the door the road is dry again,
the vicar desubstantiated. At last
we're on our own and you can tell me
how it is that you're not really dead after all.

III Piano-movers

They came like ambulance-men
in mufti, thick-soled
and trained to be careful.

Why then must he go in red blankets,
he had played it to know,
and the virus allowed to ride inside?

In one gentle tackle they had the legs
from under it. Winded, it blurted
strange harmonies and going down was still.

4

He had dreamt the last test
had come negative, though upon the keys
his Hansel-and-Gretel fingers unwove the fantastic lie.

Easing it deadweight
shoulder, they tucked the flung elbow flat
and pulled deftly on blankets and straps.

'Can't you change it?'
he'd asked of the strangers
who tended his body, but failed to reply.

Invisible neighbours watched its wheeled
passage, bumped prone down the front path
between unknown bearers.

iv Mahogany

Pressing down in twos and threes
the slack teeth of the piano's smile
I try to conjure you,
your hip knuckling against mine
for just one more shambling duet.

You do not appear: I seal
the mute mahogany. Propped
on the music-rest I read
the notes you ink-embroidered
in a song for me: Lullay, and hush.

Scattered families of notes fragment
and shimmy above their own reflections.

It's a Lovely Day Tomorrow,
you used to sing
at gilt kosher soirées. Evening
lays out along the tautened strings:

the black silk thread
along the edge of your lapel
is as clear as your face
as in the dark you stand to sing
your heart out.

Jacob Wrestles with the Angel

Squatting by the roadside I am tired,
tired to the bone of families and the road
and the river looking ready to take me.

He comes from nowhere and says nothing.
Just stands there like he's been carved out of the evening's dust
or from the hot dead reek of the rocks.

He's looking at the river. Then he starts towards me
the nowhere that he's come from hanging dark
and cool in the folds of his clothes as he moves.

I'm staring down at the road and I want to stick there
but the dust just rolls off his feet clean as marble
and I know he's come here for me.

At first I thought he was going to kiss me
his hand flat as a spade on my neck, but with the other
he's walking me into the rock.

His body is as cold as moonlight except for his hair
which is hot, and his breath at my ear. And all the time
he is looking into my face as if he owns it.

He knows the story—how I cheated my own brother.
Even with my sweat his skin is like silk as I fight him.
No one else will pass this way tonight.

We fight all night and all night I am wishing
I hadn't stolen away like that, wishing I had let them give me
a proper send-off with songs, and a harp.

Foreign Bodies

To get to where we are now in this grey
dotted area near the exploding factory or power station
we travelled like flies across four contiguous sheets

zigzagging and stopping to preen and orientate
ourselves on the spills of green hatching
the forests and fields crossed and recrossed

by the Siegfried Line and the Maginot Line
the lines of greatest and least resistance
beyond which we now live or say we do.

My hopes had been raised by two fallow deer
we passed on the roadside, stock still, a pair
inhabiting just the spot they were marked on the map

but although the room we lie down in at night
breathes in and out at the window calmly enough
the walls still do not understand a thing we say.

Amateur Radio

Fishing in the rolling dark, they cast their calls
onto the blind waves. C Q, seek you, seek you out.
Like ropes, or an arm flung out in a dream.

The ether licks at their call-signs and swallows them
whole. After such a journey near to drowning
in the earth's white air there's nobody won't let you in.

Sat together with strangers, the fat sparks fly.
Golf One Delta Zulu is beaming towards the East,
reliving the magic of hot valves and long black ebonite rods.

Seek you, seek you out. No politics or religion by law.
Appel général, appel général. I am being interfered with.
Fine business old man. George is telling us about his bees.

I am seriously troubled by static. You may make remarks
of a personal character. I am being interfered with. I'm troubled.
Fine business. We're still dead on seven three five.

And they all listen out on the singing arc for a heart-beat
of morse, for a pulse in the chhh chhh chhh. Like blood
through a stethoscope, or the sea in their ears.

In Memory of Henry West

*who lost his life in a whirlwind at the Great Western
Railway Station, Reading, March 1840, aged 24 years*

Not expecting the future in so soon, he turned
and looked for the swarm of bees. Down the lines
that had never met and never would now, it came,

the hum of the barely discernible: ribbons of flies
in a sheep down a culvert, the crack of the ice-plate
under a boot, himself in the fog.

The ironwork announced his name, then the flat
hand of the storm pushed him towards the gap.
In the eye of the wind he saw himself, halted forever

in the freezing cattle-wagon of the third class waiting room,
stopped on the table top of a Siberian winter, surrounded
by bears and the icy stares of commuters, and round him

further and further, the dopplers of a thousand 125s,
the high speed sleeper and all the other sleepers going west.

Surveillance

In operations room zero, Sergeant Joy Stick zooms
across the X-ray of the estate on her broom.
She's a smooth operator and swivels the ball in its socket
like the hip of a turkey at Christmas—nothing in it, all
done by mirrors, Lucy Locket's pocket—and locks it:
police monitor six six six. *There's a lad on a wall.*

> *We swim in the landsat of the fish-eye,*
> *pushing our prams uphill among the coral*
> *of cul-de-sacs, nosing at the dead-ends*
> *with the blunt edges of our appointment cards.*
> *From above the water they film us. At bedtime*
> *the children bury each other in the sand.*

Neighbourhood watch—eyes down for a full house.
Wild horses wouldn't drag her inside one of those:
boarded up, no self-respect. Washing their socks by night.
They're the type. She's got them in her sights—spot the ball,
spot the kid. She's smacking her lips. They're the type.
Shooting up. Take licks tonight. *There's a lad on a wall.*

> *Down here in the water it's cold as a witch's tit.*
> *We're up to something adding up to nothing*
> *and sit on the wall. In the night the great bear*
> *watches over us, it never sleeps—goodnight, kiss*
> *and William Tell. Up a bit then keep straight on*
> *till morning. We are the apple of its eye.*

The eye of the evening opens like a poppy, and the stamens
of her infra-red come pushing out like chapel hat pegs.
Here the devil hangs the dark close sheen of his tuxedo.
In the marble of her eye the yellow leaf twists and falls
and she's off across the dance-floor of rooves, foxtrot tango,
slippering the windows as she goes. *There's a lad on a wall.*

Riot

*(a 2-minute sound-piece for performance over a
recording made at an urban riot in the early 1990s)*

We moved on slowly
and heard nothing.

We knew nothing
and the boys knew that.

We lived on nothing
and the boys moved slowly.

Nothing we knew could move them.

We heard nothing we might know,
and we knew
all they were saying.

We didn't know those boys,
or what they were saying
amongst each other

how the end had been
how the end had been a relief.

And we knew
we would never move back.

Saying they had only wanted it to end
and that was that.

We didn't know those boys.
And how were we, they had said.

Nothing we heard moved us.
And how were we
to have known this was the end.

This was the end, and no messing.
To have known how it would end.

The boys moved nothing
and that was an end to it.

We heard nothing,
and that's an end to it.

On the Demolition of the Regal

We have just reached the good bit
where you and I rendezvous
on the pavement and kiss for the last time
when the ball comes crashing through
the screen, lump and tackle swinging
out over the front rows, mooning
its great derrière in the air.

My my my. Such a lot of guns
around town and so few brains.

        Your face is a room. I have lived there.

On the end of its chain the concrete
balloon gives a twirl to the balcony.
One good swing and the back row's
dragged blinking into the light
to explain itself down in the foyer.

Now let's see you do something
really tough—like putting your pants on.

        I can sit there for hours without shifting.

Plaster flowers throw themselves
in bunches onto the stage
and in the toilets rows of tiles
break out in hairline cracks,
each going crazy its own quiet way
in the dark.

Grand Hotel. Always the same.
People come, people go.
Nothing ever happens.

14

I can open the door on your breathing.

At first the old gold sticks it out,
then makes a leap and flakes down
through the wide-open air.
Whole families of dust come out
with their hands up.

I run a couple of newspapers.
What do you do?

By night your face is a cabaret show.

In the bar the optics are manacled
to the mirror with no hope of escape.
As the ball flies in from the parapet
the boys from the backroom stand firm
on the ghost of a leg and an elbow.

I have been memorising this room.
In the future I shall live a great deal
in this room.

We have switched off the lights.

Exposed to the rain, the organ
is trembling for what happens next,
her eyes on their stops wide open
with fear. For a moment King Kong
is alert to her beauty, then slings out
the ball, panning in through the swags
of her skirts as the notes hit the floor.

Close your eyes and tap your heels
together three times.

In your room in the dark you are sleeping.

The Exit signs vault for the car park
a last bid for freedom which ends
on the wires. The lamps like old troupers
pretend to be shells to the end
as the mooning balloon pirouettes
in their faces, then smacks at them
hard on the mouth.

In your room in the dark you are sleeping.

Prince Rupert's Drop

*the rapid cooling of this extraordinary glass drop
leaves it in a state of enormous tension . . .*

It's brilliant. It's a tear you can stand a car
on, the hard eye of a chandelier
ready to break down and cry like a baby, a rare
birth, cooled before its time. It's an ear
of glass accidentally sown in the coldest of water,
that sheer drop, rock solid except for the tail
or neck which will snap like sugar, kick like a mortar
under the surefire touch of your fingernail.

It's the pearl in a will-o'-the-wisp, the lantern asleep
in the ice, the light of St Elmo's fire in your eyes.
It's the roulette burst of a necklace, the snap
of bones in an icicle's finger, the snip of your pliers
at the neck of my heart, the fingertip working the spot
which says 'you are here' until you are suddenly not.

Wedding Breakfast

High
on the high table
the leaves are out
and all our fingers blossoming
with glass. The tablecloth's
a lawn, a linen bedsheet
where we lay our limbs to grass
amidst the carnival,
the cavalcade,
the mardi gras.

Your eye's a sunglass
or a solitaire, your mouth
a cave to drink the melt
which falls from my rich table.
Our lips cast burning sugar
to polish on the wind
and the table turns.

1 *The Levitation of St Christina*

*(reputed by witnesses to have flown like a bird from her coffin
during her own requiem mass—Sint-Truiden, Flanders, 1182)*

I rise on a wing and a prayer. In the aisles Father Thomas
is singing his heart out O Lamb of God all shaven and shorn
and loud enough to waken the dead. Have mercy upon us.

Up here in the gods where anything goes I am Lucifer, born
like a swan from a box, striking the light and standing well clear
of the tears, of the tar and the feathers, and of the coffin's yawn

that takest away Father Thomas's face, that waning moon
                          in the filthy air,
that gaping wound in the side of the world. And the O in his mouth
is the sins, is enough to make the angels weep. Receive
                          our prayer.

Out of the hive of the yet to be born, I'm the queen bee, behemoth
in the candle's flame, shifting my shape in the smoke dance,
the dance of death, whose sting is the needle fixed on
                          celestial north.

I leap, and my shadow's a shroud-span over the mountains,
                          an icy stroke
down the cheek of the earth. I have only to touch the hills and
                          they shall smoke.

2 The Tunnel

Ask me what it was like at the end of the tunnel,
if it was white as a moon surgeon's fingernail,
light as the water out from the crush of the wheel,
as the breast of an owl, too white to enter,
too tight a fit at the lych gate almost,
then there you are, a bride in the garden at Sissinghurst,
up at the summit of Everest, not one step further
to go, white as the snowfall of morphine,
the chalky descent to the house you were born in,
a sheet, a broken back mended, the third day, as roses?

Or was it black, another dark tunnel
crammed in the arse or mouth of the first,
your very own mine-shaft or mad-house of lost
without trace, of no face left on the shroud
to speak of or talk about, black as the bite
the earth takes out of the moon, as an axefall
of slurry, a mouthful of silence, the heart
of the slag-heap, as hungry, as no chance,
as no hope of getting a word out,
your own name forgotten, as eaten already?

3 Salvation as a Diving-Suit

The opera of her breathing fills the whole village
and even on the hillside they can hear her enlightenment
bubbling like a narghile in the mouth of God.

From inside the helmet she watches the others swim.
Shoals of bishops and other big fish nose at the glass
manifesting the dark markings of their consciences.

Saved for sure, she has to be weighted down to the sea-bed
of the market square. But sinning's smell seeps in at the seams,
a slow inundation of children's hair and used bank notes.

Her visor is cloudy with what she knows—she reels up
to the light, to the air that is promised, the towers of silence,
the blue, the sky, the burial. Walking in space.

4 St Christina Settles Down in a Convent after her Miraculous Time as a Bird

from the Prioress's journal:

I have caught her again, crooning like a sick goose
at the stones in the atrium, 'I know and am this house.'

In chapel I see her perched, listening to the wings of the moths
quivering behind the tight needlework of the altarcloth

and I know that she's flying again, that the dusty rood-screen
is a mirador, the font a fountain in some other Christ's harem

where she and the moon together go naked in the night
under their black robes, their small breasts silent and white,

their miraculous markings and silver anklets hidden, until
they fall to lie cooling in marble pools, shameless and still.

In these dark days I watch her in the refectory, pecking
at her food, one eye on the small high windows, working

out the distance, there and back again, our winter visitant.
In the tallow smoke her eye glitters with that other continent.

5 Relic

Who could stab a finger at the chest
of her childhood and say, that was the day
it arrived in the village, the stuff with X-ray eyes,
settling itself in the easy chair of her flesh,
sacred sternum, solar plexus, her future, her stars.

Worth more than gold or gems, this radiation,
spirit of the knee-cap and the finger-bone
swung like an ammeter or steeple vane in the lap
of the wind, only one place to go from here,
walking on water, dancing through fire, the next step.

The King of Portugal has her finger. Wing-tip grounded.
Shrine to the immortal possibilities of vertebrates.
Inside the trunk or chest the bones glow in the dark,
not wanted on voyage. The patellae of penitence,
the ulna and radius of flight, these are her only children.

Elbow

'women who expose their elbows, even in the sweltering heat, give their husbands sufficient reason for a divorce'—Rabbinical ruling, 1994

I am elbow, husband. I am the cup which glistens
here in the secret ruck of her sleeve,
imprinted with children, the wall of a cave.
I am also any sharp turn or change in direction

in the road. I'm an angle, a bent joint or union
where things come together. Which you husband
used to caress, to cup like a breast in a crowd,
at your mother's. Where two things join.

Out-at-elbow's a hound who is not
a straight mover. In this forbidden zone she sweats
a tiny river, a lovely lacework of salt threads
hidden. It is a weakness in the dog.

I know I am what you'd prefer to keep in the dark.
This unweathered snatch of her skin, schoolgirl thin.
The pulse of her, here where her vein
takes the blood home, the way back to her heart.

At-one's-elbow is in close attendance
just when it's needed, near at hand.
You come at her side on, an elbow wind
steering me, pushing her. Ready for use.

Out-at-the-elbows is ragged or worn
that is, threadbare. She is worn with your ragged
ebb and flow, that is, a monotonous backwards
and forwards. I am an erogenous zone.

You are not a straight mover, and I am your bitter
cup. It is a weakness in the dog. The way
back to her heart. A wind blowing sideways.
The cup you never put your lips to.

Land Girl

In the arctic dark of a winter
that's neither sleeping nor waking
she stumbles across the flank of the farm.
The cows lie like tanks in the mud,
but the field will wait till dawn
to sleep, watch one last hour
out the corner of the sky's red eye
shot with fire from Southampton.

She takes the weight of the bucket,
of the whole valley, flat out, face up,
awake all night. Gathering height
first light breathes trails of rime
along the furrows of her breeches,
there where in the pub last night
the men had fixed their pitchfork stares.

On the hills beyond the village
the lights of a decoy city go out
and in Eliot's Field the potatoes
stand at the ready, home guard
in their blind drills. Soon she will dig,
driving the fork with her hip, will drag
whole families from their beds.
The soil will turn the other cheek.

Sunrise, and the crows, unable to forget
their victories of the plague years,
are mustering in the thin grey trees.
The valley unbuttons its shirt,
the sheep stand their ground.
Down the breast of the home field
chalk runs like milk, or a prayer.

War Widow

You are buried
In the weave of your old coat-sleeves
In the stitch of your old jumpers
And in the wood-pigeons' jungle at the bottom of the garden
In the last of dusk.

You are concealed
In the mesh of every morning,
Waiting to be discovered
Like the puzzle-book bird which hangs
Upside down in the branches.

I try to concentrate
On the fixed lines: twigs, tiles and fences
Paving-stones and bricks,
The inlay of the humdrum.

But the air's weave is not so easy.
Shifting out of resolution, it insists
On pushing out your body at me:
Newsreel puppet living in the air,
A hologram in uniform.

Yesterday your ghost appearance,
Snapshot in a wartime feature, ambushed me:
My signals officer still giving out signals
After all these years.

And I knew your face
As if it were my own for me to look
Through into the camera.
Across the screen of dots I crept,
To infiltrate the ink and lie with you.

Call-Up

They are flat in the field,
in a room of yellow, making
a love out of the past and the hot sun.

In this room in the sun
they are parting and meeting again
for the first time.

Each is learning by heart,
like the intricate parts of a watch,
the face of the other.

The Tea-Makers

1

And did Muriel that night, pale as a mushroom
on the town hall roof, her father asleep at home
with only the damp sheets and passe-partout

for cover, look out over the Duke of Bedford's woods
towards the flak and the fire, imagine the damage,
the melt of ormulu clocks and bakelite radios,

witness the tilt of a parachute into its slipstream of fire,
the telegraph boys on their bicycles heading in darkness
for villages nobody knew how to spell, was the sky
over London a ladder with angels ascending, descending?

Or was it the firework display she was newsreeling in,
like a birthday or wedding, the end of a war, or the glittering
scales of the fish she had queued for since dawn then gutted
and cooked for their tea, one eye upward like a bomber's moon?

2

Has your house been touched, dear,
and the leads blown to chicken-wire?
*A piece of the dark, like shrapnel
in the daytime.* She'd have only died
worrying anyway. What with the raids,
and the jumper pinched no doubt.
A piece of time in the darkness.
Sent there for safety, all of them.
We needn't worry, now she's an angel.
A piece of time in the daylight.

3

The other wards are cellars
where the men lie like bottles
taking the true weight of the days and nights
upon themselves for others.

But here in the kingdom of shadows
where she is sister, the air is full of sentences,
like angels, invisible to the naked eye.

The men sit propped up in the dark, alert
as Lancasters, fingers flying across the pages
and once in a blue while a flutter of wings,
whole paragraphs touching down.

At her waist the keys to all their hearts
fan themselves, cooling on a lost snow-field
where her mind's eye weeps for a man
so finely tuned only she can see him.

His face lies upturned on a mountainside,
an open book which she reads alone
by night when all the lights are out.

Dior Fashion-Plate 1947

It is March on the Quai d'Orsay,
and Austerity hangs on in the trees.
A woman with Chinese eyes
is modelling the New Look.
The shantung jacket, pinched
at the waist, explodes
in a statement of liberation
over a burst of night-black pleats.

Her smile is a reflex
in the flash of the photographer's gun;
the jet of her eyes, the black shellac
of her ancestor's hair, her tiny feet,
all gifts from her mother.
The paddy-field hat is a notion
for the future, the New Order.

Her gloved hands demonstrate
the era, poised for anything—
green tea at the Hôtel George V,
rouge-et-noir at the Café Saigon,
she is yours for the bidding.
Beneath the shot silk skirt
her ivory skin flinches
against the steel of winter.

Lady Grange on St Kilda

*1732—The Edinburgh judge Lord Grange, wishing to be rid of his wife,
had her taken away and abandoned on the remote island of St Kilda*

The tide turns like a regiment for home and I am left
backstitching the day, brocading the sea for my bedspread.
In the kirkyard each unmarked stone has a different ring
so my people will know which one I'm singing in.

Tonight, the wind will come trampling the hair of the grass
dancing his twostep of profitless journeys, billowing his fist
in my face, throwing his conjuror's knives at my ear
whispering *Who, lady? Who do you think you are?*

But I shall buckle on my thistle shoes
and dance with my children the stones back out across
the blue sea holly. Then the rain will take me in her sail

to the nursery's utter west, where the moon is as pale
as a spoon, and the sun is the eye of a doll going down
and the bedcovers lift and sink with the lungs of the drowned.

No Theatre

This is the theatre of no
where the house is papered with strangers
and blue skies are grey skies
are not a rehearsal

and down at the front
it's high tide, high time
where the footlights are putting
a toe in, chancing their arm
in the great turn-around
now the ships have come in
and the cows have come home

and they're counting them in
the clown king and the roaring boys
the travesty roles, all watching
to see who's in tonight
believing they're in with a shout
or a dog's chance as if.

And don't you remember remember
how in a winter's tale or in
a boarding house along the sea-front
down a leafy lane, the statue
seemed to move, came home
to roost, where home is a stranger
who once seemed so near

as if when the shouting is over
and the stalls have quit talking
and it's all gone quiet over there
we might together ever
gather lilacs in the spring
or be in with a shout
or come home to the house again.

Theatrophone

*1911 . . . as a subscriber to this new telephonic invention,
Proust first heard Debussy's 'Pelléas et Mélisande' direct
from the Opéra Comique, while lying at home in his bed.*

In the dark electric room, the wardrobe
and the plates of cakes observe an active silence.
The past is corked into the thick air, vanishing
and returning like a harlot among the bedcovers.

He is banked on a hotbed of pillows,
buried in eiderdowns, caught in between
the minute to come which runs towards death
and the minute just passed which is dead.

Now into his ear, like the sea from a shell,
young Pelléas calls from the depths of a vault
made of cardboard: *J'étouffe* . . . The air here
is stifling. *Sentez vous l'odeur de mort?*

Sortons . . . let us leave. Pelléas in his heart
is only a boy. *Sortons* . . . he is calling. Come out.
He is destined to die but climbs out to the light
and the air of the sea: *enfin, je respire.*

The score is awash with daylight. And there
between every suck and sigh of the waves
hangs the perfume of roses. In the brackish air
of the room a memory rises and explodes:

the children go down to the sea again and again,
the sun sits in judgement, the perfume of roses
floods into his lungs. He is choking, igniting
his sharp asthma powders, transfixed.

On stage it is noon. He is fighting for breath.
A tolling of bells hammers deep in his chest,
the sea comes and goes. At the mouth of the vault
Pelléas stands full in the sun and sings.

The Cutting-Room

When the time came to consider what might
or might not be obvious to the eye,
bits of himself were already vanishing
under the knife.

Whole sections were falling like hair to the floor—
the lighter that never struck lucky first time,
the hero's best punch-lines forgotten then
tried till they hurt,

the night they went back to the river to do it
again. The clouds that had gathered when no one
was watching. The unwelcome shadow
on screen.

It was all coming out now, the gross repetitions,
the blood and the pieces of gut, the tracker dog
and the suspect's leg—just what are we
looking at now?

So he lay like a map for the generals who point
at a hilltop the audience already knows to be lost,
and watched it all backwards, the laughter, the corpsing,
the people just left coming back

and wondered which bits they'd remember,
what chance, like the piano strings broken by Liszt,
they'd fashion bracelets from the pieces left
or wear them at their wrists.

Cosmonaut 1992

The arcade scores his fifteenth orbit
of the earth today, and the silence on the radio
is crystal clear. Every two hours he passes
directly over his wife.

His body is on stand-by—
black tongues of hair break rank across his forehead
and his eyes are as dark and as deep as Lake Baikal,
absorbing all things.

At a more appropriate
moment, he will think of this as his sarcophagus.
Outside the portholes, there are more stars
than you could shake a stick at.

His mouth is set
with energy: the electrolyte of his saliva
has formed a battery between his tongue,
resting so long, and his teeth.

The earth and its oceans
are beautiful. He floats here like a baby for Unity, for Peace,
and his body is steeped in the aura
of regulation cleansing.

The power supply is unreliable
and condensation is a problem, but Progress is due,
bringing enough lunches and dinners to see him through
the next month.

He walks in the night
through the drift of his own waste which hugs the capsule.
His helmet fogs with his breathing. On the scales,
he is nothing.

He understands that Leningrad
is now St Petersburg, that living becomes harder by the day.
They will deliver him—he will search for the words,
he will appear unmoved.

The Pathologist and the National Trust

Believing the legend he's read on the map, that the tenants
used to pay their rent in feathers, that the servants
didn't know enough to come in out of the rain, he has taken
the path over the ha-ha in expectation of plenty.

But in the wisteria Weeks's Tubular Boiler is entirely lost,
and little is known in the library. *The Lord Beaconsfield*
is a splendid Melon and I like it better than any I am acquainted with.
One of the finest examples, Maud had disappeared quite suddenly.

In the still-room he dissects the thin air. A question left open,
a wound never dressed, the house has become its own attic,
a suitcase or keep-net of nothing. He leaves, taking note
of the feathers, the steps where many important have slept

or slipped unexpectedly into the net by the light of the moon,
that coin or seal on the mouth of the night, and a safe journey home.

Tita and Disraeli

*Tita: Giovanni Battista Falcieri, gondolier, brought
to England to work as steward in the Disraeli household*

In the hairy lagoon of the blankets
the flat-bottomed ham of my arm
lies parked on the bobbing meringues
of her breasts as we lie here to cool.
It's the best thing we make, this runcible pie,
the nearest we get, she and I.

Downstairs in the vegetable study, a man
who would like to be Byron but hasn't
a hope is placing the name of an enemy
inside the catacomb drawer of his desk
in the trust that something unpleasant
will happen. Young England.

In his batwing coach he creaks to Windsor,
calling on a dead man, laying his nightingales
on with a trowel, while I trail my moustachios
across the village green. Among the pyramids
of roses, I dream the sweet dancing stench
of the Lido, and the sea's sharp yawn.

There, the water smokes an opal mask
and the magistrates glide in their dragon boats
past the churches and on towards the glittering
jetties of the sultans' wives. At dinner, we have
the naming of battleships, the men stiletto
their potatoes, and the sad peas roll on to the rug.

Cook loves me, and Lord Byron died
in my arms. In the moonlight under the oaks
she will bend to collect the glow-worms
and together we will ride the galleries
and mosaics of the night, colossal and bronze
in the middle of the coldly silent lawn.

A gentleman has arrived to draw me
in chalk. I pose with fez and daggers
and spread my beard. I am John the Baptist,
Don Giovanni, Ali Baba prince of thieves.
I spit in the face of your rotting apples
and your skirts of English beef.

Summer Exhibition

The parish hall floats like a dinghy in the shadow
of St Edward and all the Martyrs. Payne's grey,
dull, recurring. Inside they unbutton their coats,
Colonel Mustard and Miss Scarlet, here for the hanging.

She heads for the regions backstage. Raw umber,
unadulterated shade. In the dark, she embraces her still life
one last time, remembers the day it all started,
two peaches and the fig she always said she couldn't give.

The others arrive with the Reverend, arranging and rearranging
objects in his head. Professor Plum, his best and closest moment
the ultramarine afternoon when he painted himself quite out
of the picture. Peacock and White, here to get out of the house.

And so they set to, nailing their colours to the mast.
The canvasses go up like sails, and soon the hall is flying
high over fields of red madder and into the wild blue yonder,
Prussia and Paris, the yellowing city of Naples, Bohemia's green.

The ship they have built wheels high above burning Sienna,
Pompeii, Berlin, above lakes brimmed with crimson,
caput mortuum's violet bruises in Rome, coming down
in the churchyard of Cyprian umber, where the pigments groan.

Dig

A quarter to ten. Under their sunhats they're looking at
                                     everything,
scraping with all the politeness of trowels at the face of the field,
tying labels to the toes of shadows, working inwards through
                                     its rings of skin.

Horizontal's the Great North Road, and vertical is a stake
                                     through the heart.
They'll work all day until their backs and fingers seize as if
                                     they'd built
the pyramids—forearms brown as bogmen, each man digs
                                     his own pit.

Stood to the waist in midden-pits and grain-stores, the eyeholes
                                     of the hill,
they are bailing stones to stop the past from sinking. The horizon
                                     will wait
and holds good. Perhaps the girl had been a warrior, the horse a
                                     dragon after all.

Four thirty. In the tea-tent the light is sitting down on the grass.
Outside, the poppies talk with their dead. The dandelion clocks
                                     and all that weight
of information take off together into the bushes.
                                     Time, gentlemen, please.

Thyme

Scientists are at this very moment
exploring the powers of thyme
to delay the ageing process.

Which would not have surprised
the ancient Romans, who understood
how well it lends itself to desiccation,
keeping its perfume long after
other herbs have faded to nothing.

Familiar with its efficacy against
nightmares, sleepless nights and pain,
they carried it on long campaigns,
basketfuls to see them through
the decimating alpine winters.

Public Footpath

Punch-bag heavy and daubed with tan
the cow's flank spasms
at the touch of a fly's front legs.

Her Bette Davis eyelashes
rake the horizon and take in
the lawyer in quality anorak
climbing the stile on his weekly stroll.

Masticating a line through the grass
the animal moves, an island
of muscle, towards the path.
She is joined by her council of sisters
and the man-corral begins.

The tearing of grass by its roots
reverberates through the solicitor's shoes.
He is spooked by the pistons of cow-breath
which drive down around him

and has just time to note
the NHS pink of the animal's lips
and the muscled blue rasp of her tongue
before she lies down on him.

While she rolls her meat on him,
the eyes of her sisters deadpan
and connive at the ringside.
He'll be lucky if he walks away from this.

Ogress

Pie-eyed and sinning already with her tongue
she crosses herself and the glutinous act,
the grubfest, can begin. Stewed in their own juices
the little limbs slew on the spoon.

Granny is wolfing her offspring down,
hooking them down, her flesh and her blood.
These are their bodies and something is eating her.
Tender as the morning, and so pretty.

Here in Castle Dangerous where waking is sleeping
Baroness Orco eats standing up in the dark,
shovelling snow into the mouth of the burning cave,
eating their hearts out, scarfing them up.

The babies slither into her womb
like stones into the belly of the wolf dragged
to the cold of the river, the invisible region
where eating is hunger and anything's food.

The children have gone down like lambs
and she is face to face with the beast,
with the act of commital. Like so much muck
before the shovel. The spectre at the feast.

Timed Exposure

At the eleventh hour in the empty quarter
we stand and watch our shadows
spinning on the clock face of the sand.

We are the dunes, the Chiltern hundreds,
ash and lilac, oak and beech wood
made by all the women of your family.

Our room is as full as a quarrel, as empty
as a child with the windows out. Clouds
of our old clothes race across the floor.

We are not even the stars. The lid of our house
is off, and in the lava trail of tail-lights on the hill
we must make all our journeys over again.

The First Week

Seven times I will look down
from my window to check the latest state
of the truth: you are not here.
You have been painted out, the step
between the gateposts perfectly retouched.

Seven times I will lie down
on this whitewash of a sheet
next to the neat scissors job
of your absence. You are not here,
you are not here.

Seven times I will go down
to the yellow field. From the place where you lay,
your body has been scythed and every flower-head
restored. Even the bend of your shadow.
You are not here.

We All Know that You're Going

We all know that you're going—
we have seen you in the body
that you still put about, at the school gates
and shopping for the freezer
as if you were staying.

Your disguise as one of us
is wearing thin. Held up to the light
you have become a Chinese parasol
unfurled, spectacular, daring
the wind to come and take you.

In the flat of the morning
and in the changing rooms we talk
about you. Hounded out of your chest,
legs confiscated, you have holed up
in the palace of your face.

We all know that you're going—
your coat hung up behind the door,
the footprints that you leave beside the bath,
the breath you plume into the air,
do not convince us.

Bathrooms

1

Your washbag and its siamese twin
are the only props in the photo you took
of yourself alone in the limp Crete winter.

Cut off at the hips, you continue
to smile and grapple to be free
of the camera that blindfolds your face.

The little of you that remains to view
is encased in a courtyard of tiles,
the ceramic remains of a settlement.

2

One particular friend's bathroom
is now a poison-cupboard, spiked as it is
with the same almond-and-primrose oils
they used to veil the smell of your exhaustion.

Contemptuous of this flimsy purdah
the virus of course had continued
to dance and trick from room
to room, confident of conquest.

3
For thirty five years I have had
my reflection to myself.
Now I have to share it
with your shade, coming in
without knocking before even
the tea is made, the night seen off.

Trident Papa India

June 18, 1972 Trident Papa India fell from the sky, minutes after leaving
the airport, into a meadow only 400 yards from Staines High Street.

In photos from newscuttings Aerospace Minister Heseltine's hair
looks coquettishly long, and policemen appear to embrace
souvenir-

hunters. One man drove from Kent. 'There've been scores
of them, coming with sandwiches, scaling my fences since dawn,'
reports

Miss Alice Gent. From our blue-marbled steering wheel,
Father had guessed
their real interest, to view at close quarters the death they'd just
missed.

The fall of spaghetti from heart monitor to his chest some
five years
later brought it back to me. That same messed skein of wires,

the mime-show of rescue and salvage work around the bed,
the trace of violet and blue along his feet the night he died.

My mother kept the car and drove it out on winter nights
collecting us from parties. 'There are days,' the pilot's wife

had said when interviewed, 'when it is all that I can do
to turn the kids' fish fingers in the pan.' The journeys home

were awkward. Wincing at the difficult fan of screen
she fathomed our way back for us, almost a husk with grief.

Admission

In my mother's empty bedroom
the plush of dust on the venetian blind
filtered the light outside to almost nothing,
the past as soon as it hits the slats.

Next day we kicked our way amongst the litter
of dementia to the Ellen Terry nissen hut
and found her happy, a schoolgirl working
on a project on Open Day when the family turn up.

How soon she learned to hide
in the horseshoe of nodding doll-heads,
each cleverly disguised in makeshift hairstyles
and the cardigans of the deceased.

Radcliff Patterson and Symons, Radcliff
Patterson and Symons: they were chums, she said
and went on counting, one to a hundred
and back, her break-neck jamming of the hours.

In the day-room she watches Sportsnight
with all the scrutiny of a pundit and deliberately
throws both halves of her dentures into the gloom
of dust, collecting like velvet behind the radiator.

What matters

is the way we lived: you tying the laces
on each school day, gripping the shoulders
of your bike lest it move off alone and leave you

you on your hunkers by the kitchen fire
performing surgery on the hoover
difficult and slack-heavy as a teenager

your notebook copper-plated with the whole
Our Father, suppliers of discontinued kitchen parts
and our impossibly distant addresses

then the last of the picnics, *Travels with a Donkey*,
the sweet years turning over and over
and you falling asleep as I read.